What Is a Fish?

by Lola M. Schaefer

chain moray

Consulting Editor: Gail Saunders-Smith, Ph.D.

Consultant: Dwight Lawson, Ph.D.
General Curator, Zoo Atlanta

Pebble Books

an imprint of Capstone Press
Mankato, Minnesota

Pebble Books are published by Capstone Press
151 Good Counsel Drive, P.O. Box 669, Mankato, Minnesota 56002
http://www.capstone-press.com

1 2 3 4 5 6 06 05 04 03 02 01

Library of Congress Cataloging-in-Publication Data
Schaefer, Lola M., 1950–
    What is a fish?/by Lola M. Schaefer.
    p. cm—(The Animal Kingdom)
    Includes bibliographical references (p. 23) and index.
    ISBN 0-7368-0865-5
    1. Fishes—Juvenile literature. [1. Fishes.] I. Title. II. Series.
QL617.2 .S33   2001
597—dc21   00-009670

Summary: Simple text and photographs present fish and their general characteristics.

Note to Parents and Teachers

The Animal Kingdom series supports national science standards
related to the diversity of living things. This book describes the
characteristics of fish and illustrates various kinds of fish. The
photographs support early readers in understanding the text. The
repetition of words and phrases helps early readers learn new
words. This book also introduces early readers to subject-specific
vocabulary words, which are defined in the Words to Know section.
Early readers may need assistance to read some words and to use
the Table of Contents, Words to Know, Read More, Internet Sites,
and Index/Word List sections of the book.

Table of Contents

Fish 5
Parts of a Fish 11
Swimming 17

Words to Know 22
Read More 23
Internet Sites 23
Index/Word List 24

largemouth bass in fresh water

koran angelfish in salt water

Fish are part of
the animal kingdom.
Some fish live in fresh
water. Some fish live
in salt water.

Fish are cold-blooded.
Their body temperature
is the same as the
water around them.

southern stingray

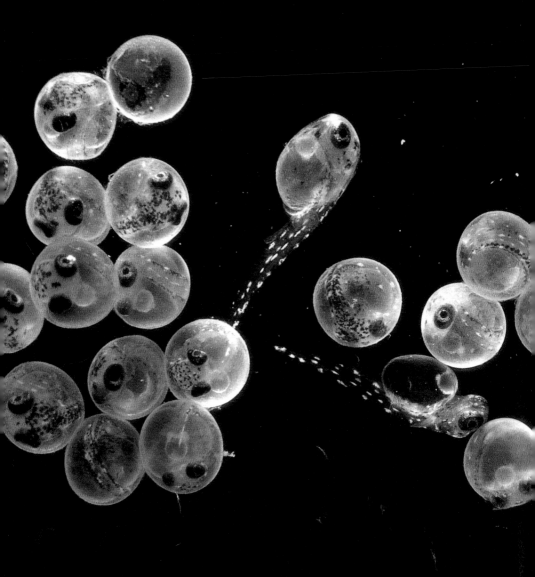

Most fish lay eggs.
Young fish hatch
from eggs.

fish eggs and hatching young

Fish have a skeleton.

crucian carp

Fish have scales.

giant perch

Fish breathe through gills.

whitetip reef shark

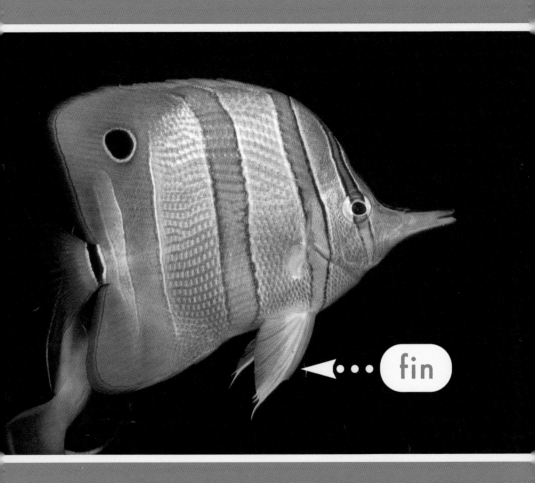

fin

Fish have fins to help
them swim.

butterfly fish

Fish move their tail back and forth to swim.

goldfish

Some fish swim together
in groups called schools.

school of goat fish

cold-blooded—having a body temperature that is the same as the temperature of the surroundings; fish, reptiles, and amphibians are cold-blooded animals.

fin—a body part of a fish that is shaped like a flap; fish use fins to swim, turn, slow down, and stop.

fish—a cold-blooded animal that lives in water; fish have scales, fins, and gills; more than 20,000 kinds of fish live in the world.

fresh water—water that does not have salt; most ponds, rivers, lakes, and streams have fresh water.

gill—a body part used to take oxygen from water; fish live underwater and use gills to breathe.

salt water—water that has a lot of salt; water in oceans and seas is salt water.

scales—small pieces of hard skin that cover the body of a fish or reptile

Read More

Kalman, Bobbie, and Allison Larin. *What Is a Fish?* The Science of Living Things. New York: Crabtree Publishing, 1999.

Savage, Stephen. *Fish.* What's the Difference? Austin, Texas: Raintree Steck-Vaughn, 2000.

Stewart, Melissa. *Fishes.* A True Book. Danbury, Conn.: Children's Press, 2001.

Internet Sites

Ask Shamu: Fish
http://www.seaworld.org/ask_shamu/fish.html

Fish
http://www.factmonster.com/ce6/sci/A0818770.html

Fish
http://www.wh.whoi.edu/faq/index.html

What Is a Shark?
http://www.EnchantedLearning.com/subjects/sharks

Index/Word List

animal
  kingdom, 5
body, 7
breathe, 15
cold-blooded, 7
eggs, 9
fins, 17
fresh water, 5
gills, 15

groups, 21
hatch, 9
help, 17
lay, 9
live, 5
most, 9
move, 19
salt water, 5
scales, 13

schools, 21
skeleton, 11
swim, 17, 19, 21
tail, 19
temperature, 7
through, 15
together, 21
water, 7
young, 9

Word Count: 77
Early-Intervention Level: 7

Editorial Credits
Mari C. Schuh, editor; Kia Bielke, cover designer and illustrator; Kimberly Danger,
  photo researcher

Photo Credits
Dwight R. Kuhn, 8
Jane Burton/Bruce Coleman Inc., 10
J. C. Carton/Bruce Coleman Inc., cover (upper right), 18
Ralf Astrom/Bruce Coleman Inc., 1
Ron & Valerie Taylor/Bruce Coleman Inc., 20
Tom & Terisa Stack/Tom Stack & Associates, 6
Tom Brakefield/Bruce Coleman Inc., cover (lower left)
Visuals Unlimited/Hal Beral, cover (upper left); Maslowski, cover (lower right);
  S. Maslowski, 4 (top); Alex Kerstitch, 4 (bottom); Ken Lucas, 12;
  David B. Fleetham, 14; Bill Kamin, 16